BUBBY, ME, AND MEMORIES

Barbara Pomerantz

Photographs by LEON LURIE

Union of American Hebrew Congregations
New York, New York

Special thanks to:

Rabbi Daniel B. Syme • Stuart L. Benick • Steven Schnur
Rabbi Howard I. Bogot • Josette Knight • Dr. Jack Horowitz
Ronald Mass • Rabbi Gerald M. Kane • Rabbi Kenneth D. Roseman
Deborah Reshotko • Dr. Lenore Sandel • Rabbi Alan D. Fuchs

This book is dedicated to the
beauty of my Bubby and to
my daughters, Shari and Deborah,
who remember her well...

Foreword

Every year since I started teaching, parents have come to me asking for a way to help their children understand death. In my efforts to guide them, I found too few good books for the young Jewish child. Though I could never claim that this book, *Bubby, Me, and Memories*, is the answer, it is, at least, a beginning. Perhaps it will help all of us to think more about that inevitable fact of life which we call death. Though death is a universal experience, we each confront it in a very personal way . . . but confront it we must. Even very young children are not immune from feeling a deep sense of loss.

When children ask questions, they need answers. When children feel grief, they need comfort. When children see us mourn, they need our open permission to comfort us. When children are curious about death, they need to be shown the purpose of life. Perhaps that is the real reason for this book. Our immortality is in the memories we leave behind.

My thanks to Rabbi Jay Karzen, spiritual leader of Maine Township Jewish Congregation, Des Plaines, Illinois, and to Marvell Ginsburg, early childhood consultant with the Chicago Board of Jewish Education, for their guidance; to Belle Wagner and Donna Strauss for their beautiful faces; to Sherwin Pomerantz for his sharing and caring; and, most of all, my deepest gratitude to Bubbies everywhere.

This is a picture of my Bubby and me.
Some kids call their Bubby Grandma.
Some kids call their Bubby Nana.
I always called my Bubby Bubby.

I remember the times Bubby took me to the park,

and walked with me,

and hugged me.

I remember the times Bubby read to me.
Her favorite stories were from the Bible.
Once I surprised her with a puppet I made.
It was Joseph. I even made him a coat.
Bubby liked the colors.

I remember the times Bubby brought me presents
and it wasn't even Chanukah!

Bubby and I baked chalah together
and she told me funny jokes
while we ate the warm bread.

Bubby sang to me.
I learned her lullaby a long time ago
when I was only three.

A few days ago my Bubby died.

When Daddy told me about Bubby,
I felt like crying.
Daddy said it's okay to cry.
Pretty soon the sad part of me
won't hurt so much.

I don't know why my Bubby had to die.
I guess even my Mommy and Daddy don't know.
They told me everything that is alive
dies some day.
That means old people and very, very sick people,
and plants, and animals.

I thought maybe Bubby is asleep
for a little while,
and she'll wake up again.
Daddy said Bubby is not asleep.
Bubby will not wake up again.
That isn't what happens when someone is dead.

I asked Mommy if Bubby went away.
Mommy and Daddy went away one time.
They went to Israel on a big airplane.
Then they came back.
Mommy said Bubby did not go on a trip.
Bubby died.
She is never, ever coming back.

There is a big candle in the living room.
It's taller than a birthday candle.
It's wider than a Shabbat candle.
We will light one every day for seven days.
We will be together with my aunts and uncles
and cousins for seven days.
That's called sitting shivah.

A lot of people are in the living room.
Mrs. Cohn is here. She's our neighbor,
and she was Bubby's good friend.
Mrs. Cohn misses Bubby.
Mr. Curtis, my Daddy's boss, is here.
He takes me to the circus every year.
Mr. Curtis is our friend.
Mrs. Levy, the president of the PTA at school, is here.
Mommy helps her. She wants to help Mommy.

They all know we feel lonely without Bubby.

I sit in my room and think about Bubby.
Then Daddy takes me with him to the synagogue.
I hold a prayer book. I see the rabbi.
There are other people there.
Some of them feel sad like me.
Somebody they loved died too.
They say a special Hebrew prayer called Kaddish.
My Daddy says Kaddish too.
I listen to him.
I think about Bubby.

I know I'll always remember Bubby.
I'll always think about her a lot.
When Mommy and I light candles on Friday night,
I think about Bubby.
She taught me the special Hebrew blessing.
I used to say ''Baruch a toy.'' Bubby would smile.
Everybody would smile.
But that isn't the right way.
''Baruch atah'' is the right way.
Now I'm bigger.
I know the right words.
Everybody still smiles when I say the prayer.

I remember Bubby when I look
into her old mirror on her dresser.
Everybody tells me I look like Bubby.
That makes me feel happy.

Sometimes when I think about Bubby,
I feel lonely.
I take out this picture
of the two of us and hold it.
I remember all the things
we used to do together,
and I begin to feel better.
I really love my Bubby.
And I always will.

246.5 J
Pom